Basketball's Balanced Offense

Jim Harrick

MASTERS PRESS

A Division of Howard W. Sams & Company

Masters Press (A Division of Howard W. Sams & Co.)
2647 Waterfront Parkway, East Drive, Suite 300
Indianapolis, IN 46214

Library of Congress Cataloging-in-Publication Data

Harrick, Jim, 1938-
Basketball's balanced offense / Jim Harrick.
      p. cm.
    ISBN: 1-57028-023-1: $12.95
     1. Basketball--Offense
     I. Title

GV889.H357 1995
796.323'2 – dc20   95-18747
                                                  CIP

Credits:
Cover design by Phil Velikan
Diagram reproduction by Christy Pierce and Kelli Ternet
Edited by Kim Heusel
Photographic reproduction by Terry Varvel
Editorial assistance by Holly Kondras
Text layout by Kim Heusel

Acknowledgments

To John Wooden, from whom I have learned so much. Ditto Pete Newell.

To Al Ball, Pud Hutson, Jules Rivlin and Sonny Moran — coaches I played for who gave me a foundation of fundamentals.

Also, Lee Smelser, Dutch Belnap, Rod Tueller, Gary Cunningham, Larry Farmer, Tom Asbury, Graig Impelman, and all the coaches I have served with and who have been assistants for me, especially current ones Mark Gottfried, Lorenzo Romar and Steve Lavin.

I particularly owe a tremendous debt to the 12 members of the 1994-95 UCLA national championship basketball team:

Ed O'Bannon

Tyus Edney

George Zidek

Kevin Dempsey

Ike Nwankwo

Kris Johnson

Cameron Dollar

Bob Myers

Toby Bailey

omm'A Givens

J.R. Henderson

Charles O'Bannon

Introduction

I believe with all my heart the ability to win basketball games is based on how well a team plays defense from the top of the key to the baseline, and how well the offense is executed from the top of the key to the baseline.

The Balanced Court Offense isn't the only offense in the world, but I believe it's the best. It provides balanced and triangle rebounding, and medium and deep safeties. The basic Guard Cut Play is from Coach John Wooden while the other segments of the offense are from Coach Gary Cunningham.

I used the offense at Morningside High School but really learned the intricacies while an assistant coach at UCLA under Gary Cunningham. I ran it nine years at Pepperdine University and currently at UCLA. I believe it was a real source for getting me where I am today.

It allows for the high-low, single and double screens, screen-and-rolls, the give-and-go, screens off and on the ball, splits, and all other parts of the game that help a team get baskets.

I watched John Wooden win 10 national championships, Denny Crum win two, and last year our UCLA team won the title. The beauty of the offense is that a coach can design his own plays to the personnel he has.

There are usually equal shots for all positions, but the cream will rise to the top. I tell my players that our offense will get them a good shot, but it's up to them to make it.

Jim Harrick

Former UCLA coach John Wooden, left, shares a moment with current coach Jim Harrick. Wooden won 10 national championships while coaching the Bruins. Harrick's 1994-95 UCLA team was the first to win a national title since Wooden retired in 1975.

Foreword

One of the things I like about Jim Harrick's system is its simplicity and versatility. From a teaching standpoint, it is not a complicated system. It has already been very successful in the college game and it can even help coaches at the junior and senior high school levels.

Jim's system reflects his longtime experience and knowledge of the game of the basketball. He entered the coaching ranks more than 30 years ago as an assistant at Morningside High School in Inglewood, Calif. After five years, he became the head coach and rose to become one of the nation's most successful high school coaches at the time.

Following his high school career, Jim became an assistant coach at Utah State and later UCLA. After paying his dues as an assistant, he became head coach at Pepperdine in 1979 and was very successful before becoming head coach at UCLA in 1988.

Jim Harrick is now entering his eighth season in Westwood and his Bruins are the defending NCAA champions. Throughout his career, Jim has never lost contact with his roots from the high school level to the summit of the college game.

I have felt for a long time that there is more overcoaching than undercoaching. Coach Harrick covers all of the details very well in his system, keeping good floor balance offensively and defensively. At the same time, he doesn't make it too difficult.

I like Jim's system very much. Some might say a lot of his offense is similar to what I used. Well, the philosophy is somewhat similar, but there is nothing wrong with that.

John Wooden, former UCLA head coach

Table of Contents

Key to Diagram Markings

Shown below are the basic symbols used in the diagrams found throughout this book. The arrow indicates the direction of movement of the player or ball.

Solid line: Player moving without the ball.

Jagged line: Player dribbling the ball.

Line with bar at end: Player setting a screen. (Screens may also be set after dribbling, passing or cutting.)

Player making a V-cut.

Player passing the ball.

1

The Balanced Court
High-Post Offense

The Balanced Court High-Post Offense was developed by Ward "Piggy" Lambert of Purdue. But it was one of his best students, three-time Purdue all-American John Wooden, who perfected it during a 40-year coaching career highlighted by 10 national titles at UCLA.

There are many offenses a coach can use, but in my opinion, the balanced court high-post is the best. It provides the necessary balanced spacing needed and numerous options: ball reversal, triangle rebounding with a medium and a deep safety on every play, and excellent pressure releases.

We want all five of our players moving at the same time. It's especially important that the players on the weak side keep their men busy at all times.

We start the offense with a guard-to-guard pass. We try to take what the defense give us and score as a direct result of a pass. The ball shouldn't stick in a player's hand for more than 1 to 1½ seconds. We want to score one-third of the time in our half-court set offense, one-third of the time on our fast break and one-third of the time on half- and full-court defensive turnovers, early offense, offensive rebounds, foul shots, out-of-bounds plays and any other opportunity that becomes available. Our opponent may succeeed in stopping one of these scoring methods, but hopefully we will succeed with another method.

The beauty of the Balanced Court High-Post Offense is that a coach can design his own plays around the strengths of his players. For example, on Hit the Post, there are a number of superb play designs possible. Every play can be run to fit the players because the coach designs it. The offense provides a team with structure.

To be effective on offense, a team must be well drilled in passing, catching, pivoting, dribbling and all other fundamentals that make the game simple and easy, but hard to perfect. If a team is plagued by turnovers, it should go back to the basics.

We believe that a team must "share the ball," play together and make the extra pass in order to win. It seems that the teams that make an effort to make the extra pass win.

We try to shoot 52-55 percent from the field in every game. We also have a goal of making 20 to 25 assists. If some of those assists come on the fast break they'll lead to easy baskets and improve our shooting percentage.

Basic UCLA Fundamentals

To be good, you must quickly and properly execute the following fundamentals of the game of basketball, what we refer to as **The Big 5.** You must be doing each one to perform properly.

Success in the Balanced Court Offense begins with the proper stance.

1. Stance

Start with feet pointed straight ahead and spread about shoulder-width. Get down, bending at the knees, not the waist, with chest out, back straight and chin up. Widen your base by 2 feet (two steps) or more. Get your buttocks down almost as if you are sitting in a chair and the chair is taken away. This is the way the game of basketball is played. ***Straight-legged players sit on the bench!***

4

In an actual game situation, UCLA's Ed O'Bannon demonstrates the intensity and determination necessary to play effective defense. Notice how O'Bannon is in the proper stance with his arms out, knees slightly bent and his feet spread to provide a wider base.

| (A) | (B) | (C) |

On offense, the ball goes on the chest, touching it under the chin with the elbows out. On defense, do what you are comfortable with. (See above photos)

1. Elbows on the ribs, the palms of the hands up, hands and arms move and the head is still. (A)
2. Dig with one hand and trace the ball with the other. (B)
3. Arms out and up, and always flashing in the passing lane. (C)

2. Concentration

To me, basketball is a very serious business. When players step across the line, they must have total concentration for the duration of practice — concentration on properly executing the *Fundamentals of the Game.*

Success in athletics depends on a player's ability to concentrate, focus and zero in on the task at hand. You shouldn't have to tell your players over and over and over — but do it anyway! Keep hammering it into them.

Think **Concentrate** **Execute**

3. Quickness

At UCLA, we feel the two most important things in basketball are *quickness* and *balance.* We try to think quickly, pass quickly, move quickly, shoot quickly, make quick outlet passes and dribble quickly. After a while, if we keep working on all of these things, we might become quick. Everything we do, we try to do quickly. Our stance and footwork drills are done daily.

Caution: Be quick — but don't be in a hurry.

Here is the fine line we call **poise:** Quickly and properly executing the fundamentals of the game while staying on balance. Basketball remains the same at all levels, but the game's quickness escalates as the level you play on is elevated.

4. Balance

Balance is described as the head at the midpoint of your two feet in everything you do.

A player who is in the proper balance will have his head located in an area midway between his two feet as this player does.

- When you **RUN,** your head must be in the middle of the two feet.
- When you **SHOOT,** your head must be in the middle of the two feet.
- When you **DRIBBLE,** your head must be in the middle of the two feet.
- When you **REBOUND,** your head must be in the middle of the two feet.
- When you **DEFEND,** your head must be in the middle of the two feet.

If the coach says "Don't Reach," he really means don't let your head get out of that midpoint. ***Balanced players play; unbalanced players ride the pine.***

5. Play Hard

The definition of hard is:

■ Your whole shirt is wet — not just part of it.

■ Your gut is pulsating.

■ You are gasping for breath!

Play hard! Your players won't break or die. Push them to their limits. Some players, especially young ones, have never gone as hard as they can.

Seven Fundamental Areas of Improvement

These basic fundamentals are essential to properly execute any offense. A player who makes these seven areas a habit will become better and his team will be much improved.

1. Acknowledge a Good Pass

When a teammate's pass to you results in a basket, you must acknowledge him. Point to him (my favorite), say "thank you," make eye contact and nod, or slap hands (I dislike this one but accept it.) The important thing is to let your teammate know you appreciate the pass. If he passes to you, you will pass to him and the *esprit de corps* on your team will be greatly strengthened. (If he never passes to you, you will never pass to him and your team will be very selfish.)

When you receive a pass from a teammate that allows you to score, acknowledge that player by pointing, nodding or making eye contact. Let him know you appreciate the pass. This goes a long way toward building unselfish team play.

2. Ball Placement

Hold the ball under the chin touching your chest with the elbows out. You should be able to slide the ball to the right or left, or down to the hip area while it is touching your chest or midsection. The key is keeping the ball against your body. If the ball is held away from the chest 6 to 8 inches it could be slapped away for a turnover. Make it touch.

3. Jump Stop

While dribbling with the ball, we want all our players to complete an even-footed jump stop, on balance and under control.

4. Follow your Shots

We encourage our players to follow their shots to the broken line to ensure that we have triangle rebounding position.

5. Hands Up on All Shots

We drill our athletes to have their hands up on every shot. This is done to ensure that each player is as big as possible and is ready to rebound no matter where the ball comes from.

6. V-Cut and Ask for the Ball

Whenever our players come to meet a pass, we like them to fake away with a short jab step (V-Cut) and ask for the ball with a hand held high to serve as a target. This keeps the defensive player off balance and forces the offensive player to meet every pass.

When meeting a pass, players should make a short V-Cut (left) and then ask for the ball, using a hand as a target for the passer (right).

7. Step-back and Crossover Dribble

When bringing the ball upcourt against extreme defensive pressure, we place our bodies between the ball and the defensive player while keeping the ball at knee level and shuffling our legs to protect it.

When changing directions:

Take a giant step back with the rear foot and drop the front foot back to the same level.

Change hands with the ball on a crossover dribble. Bring the opposite leg up to separate the ball from the defender with your body.

By protecting the ball with your body and keeping your head up at all times, anyone can advance the ball against pressure.

UCLA guard Tyus Edney brings the ball downcourt for the Bru-ins.

2

Getting Open
in the
Balanced Court Offense

The balanced court high-low post offense provides a team with every possible offensive opportunity. Any player can be posted. You can also develop a high-low game, run screen-and-rolls, run two- and three-man games, run clearouts, and set single and double screens.

One of the best aspects of this offense is it can be effective regardless of the team's overall size or the size of the center.

This offense thrives on good open shots, and our players know the offense will get them a shot. All they have to do is make it. It's important, however, that each player understand what a good shot is for him. You don't want to take a good shot and turn it into a bad play.

> *"The notoriety of the coach is dictated by the execution of his team under pressure."*
> —**Hubie Brown, former NBA coach of the year**

Part of our philosophy in basketball instruction is to teach "part" of what you want to cover to reach the "whole" of what you want covered. In other words, break down your offense into one-, two-, three- and four-man segments to help your players understand the purpose behind certain drills. To successfully run any offense, your players must learn how to "get open."

Points to Ponder

- Teach what you know; know what you teach.
- Taking the pressure off the players helps eliminate human error.
- A one-handed tip is a five percent shot; a two-handed tip is a 95 percent shot.
- Be quick but don't be in a hurry.

Moves to Get the Forwards Open

We like to start with our forwards one step out and one step up from the block. The forward V-cuts to the basket (left, below) then flashes quickly to the free-throw line extended coming to a jump stop with the inside foot up and asking for the ball (right).

The forward takes a short jab step or V-Cuts to the basket, then flashes back to the free-throw line extended and asks for the ball.

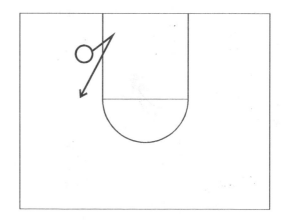

Upon receiving the pass, he may make one of three pivots — a front pivot on the inside foot and face the basket, or if overplayed by the defense, he may reverse pivot and take a one- or two-bounce dribble to the basket, jump stop and shoot a bank shot or . . .

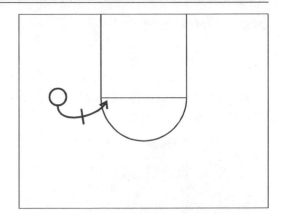

. . . reverse pivot and face the basket.

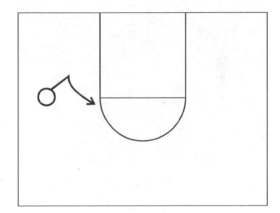

If he cannot get open, the forward V-cuts to the basket then flashes back to the junction of the foul line and foul lane where he stops. This will cause the defense to also stop. The forward then moves quickly to the free-throw line extended where he pivots and faces the basket.

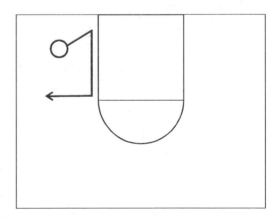

The forward starts at the free-throw line extended. If our scouting report says the opponent is a helpside-ballside defensive team we start the offense with a guard-to-guard pass. The forward V-cuts to the basket and steps through with his leg and arm. (See Step-Through)

Step-Through

The following photos and diagrams show the forward in different areas of the court executing a V-cut and throwing his hand, arm and leg through the defensive player. In all areas that you wish to get open, this maneuver with a strong V-cut will help.

V-Cut and Step-Through

Step-Through

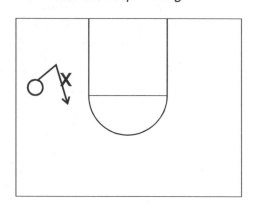

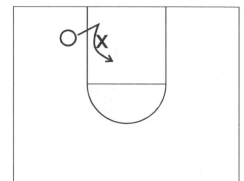

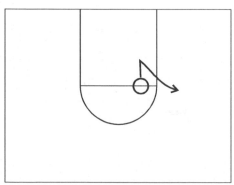

Moves to Get the Guards Open

Our guards start one step out from the free-throw lane line and one step from the top of the key. We like to start our offense with a guard-to-guard pass-dribble into the operational area and a jump stop. We fake a pass to the forward then make a pass to the other guard.

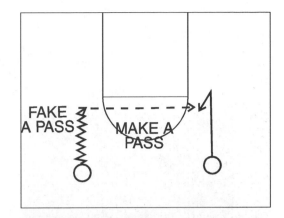

The opposite guard moves one or two steps and V-cuts a step back where he catches the ball in the jump stop position, pivots, fakes a pass to the forward then makes a pass to the other guard. The other guard does the same.

Moves to Get the Center Open

The center starts one step on the strong or ball side or he could start in the middle of the post area and step up. As the ball is passed guard to guard he steps to the strong side. As the ball is passed guard to forward, the center pivots and sets a position screen with his hands on his knees (see photos below). He then has a four-step motion to get open.

1. Pivot and set a position screen.

2. V-cut to go backdoor.

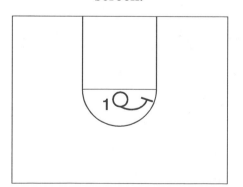
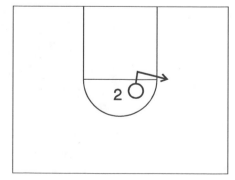

3. Step through with his arm and leg to face the forward.

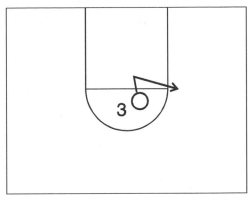

4. Catch the ball and reverse pivot facing the basket.

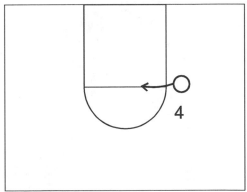

Post Moves

We like to post up with both feet above the block, body straight, knees slightly bent with a very high target hand and a bent "L"-shaped pin hand. From here, several offensive moves on the block are possible.

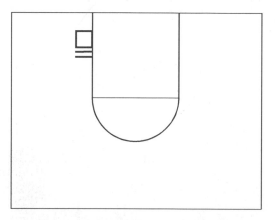

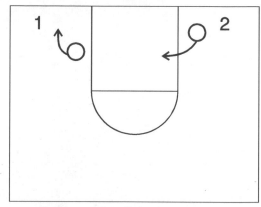

1. Turn baseline for a jump shot off the backboard.

2. Turn to the middle for a jump shot off the backboard.

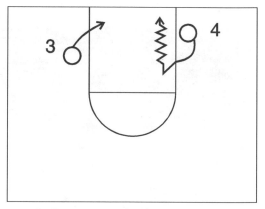

3. Drop step to the basket, a one-bounce crab dribble and power layin.

4. Front pivot and pump fake, one bounce to the basket and a power layin.

5. Hook shots left and right to the baseline and to the middle.

Pinning

In today's game, a player must learn to pin or seal his defender. We want to:

- Chop down on the defensive player's deny hand.
- Step and put the buttocks on the defender's thigh.

We work on this every day.

On the pass, step into the player. Pin him by getting his defensive arm down and holding it.

Pin and seal the defender by stepping into him and putting the buttocks against his thigh.

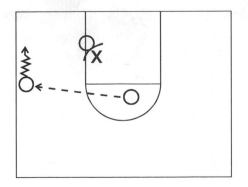

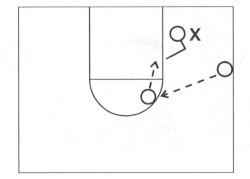

Power Move Series

Our Power Move Series is designed to help players develop moves around the basket, keep their feet still, and most of all, finish the play. In everything we do, we emphasize the importance of making the second shot if the first one is missed. Our Power Move Series is divided into three sections:

1. ***Power Moves***
2. ***Speed Moves***
3. ***Hesitation Moves***

Power Moves

Power Layin

In a stance with one foot back and his arms up, the player tosses the ball across the board. He takes a step and goes as high as possible. The second player rebounds the ball and powers up with his back to the foul line, shooting the ball as close to the glass and as high up on the glass as he can.

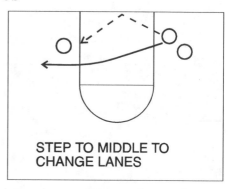

STEP TO MIDDLE TO
CHANGE LANES

Make every shot. We make one on each side.

Pump Fake Power Layin

This is set up the same as the Power Layin except after the rebound, the second player pump fakes with the ball — showing the ball in the air but keeping his feet still — followed by the power layin.

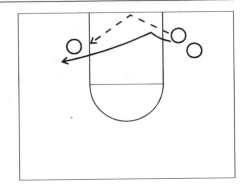

Pump Fake, 1 Bounce to Other Side, Power Layin

Again, the same setup. After the rebound, the player pump fakes, makes a one-bounce dribble to the other side of the lane where he completes the power layin.

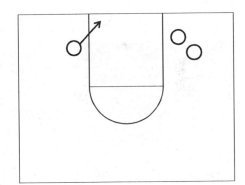

Pogo

Same setup as before but after the rebound the player keeps his arms extended and immediately goes back up with the ball as quickly as possible similar to the action of a pogo stick.

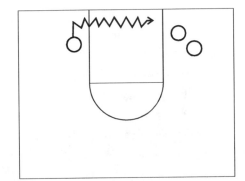

Two-Hand Follow Shot

While in the air after the rebound with both hands holding the ball, shoot a two-handed follow shot off the glass.

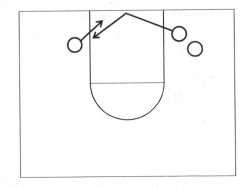

Speed Moves

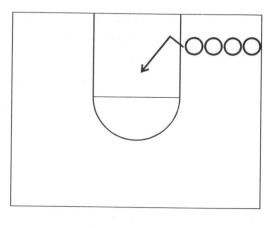

While alternating sides, players make strong V-cuts and flash into the post area with both hands up asking for the ball. When a player receives the ball, he makes a speed move to shoot without dribbling or pump faking. The player follows his shot with his hands up. He must rebound the shot if it misses and finish the play with a power series move before ball touches floor unless he gets a long bounce. One exception: If the ball goes in the basket, you can allow it to hit the floor.

In the Speed Move Drill, players V-Cut and flash into the post area (above) with both hands up asking for the ball (right).

Hesitation Moves

This is the same setup as the Speed Move Series. The difference: In this series the player pump fakes and/or makes a one-bounce dribble before taking his shot.

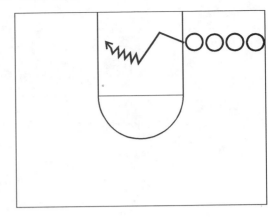

Flatten or Curl

Every offense must involve what we call flatten or curl. You can't be a good player until you see or read what is happening on the floor and get a mental picture of how a move or series is developing. The offensive player must read how the defender is going to guard him. The defender must either trail the screen (follow offensive player) or step behind the screener to meet the offensive player "at the pass." To avoid this, we "flatten or curl" the offensive player depending on what the defense gives us. In the following diagrams, X is the defensive player; O is the offensive player.

If the defensive player (31) stays with the offensive player (far right) and goes under the screen set by No. 25, then the other offensive player "curls" to the basket. The offensive player "flattens out" if the defender goes over the screen.

In the photo and in the top left diagram, if X (middle) follows O (left) under the screen (right), O curls to the basket. In the diagram below, X goes over the top of the screen. When this happens, O flattens out.

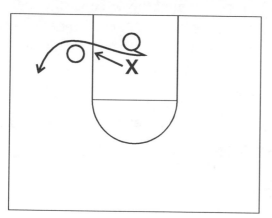

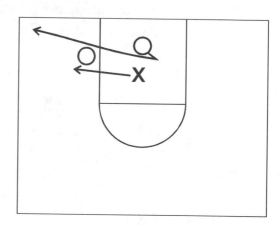

The two diagrams below show the same principle in the motion game.

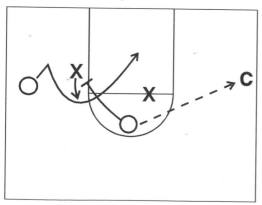

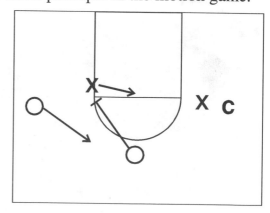

Side Post

In the balanced court high-post offense, the Guard Cut Series, which we cover later, ends up looking like this after the first pass:

2, 3 and 5 are working a three-man game on one side of the floor.

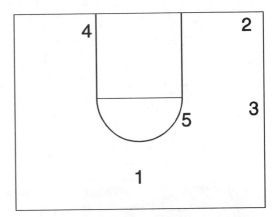

1 and 4 (on a reverse pass by 3) are ready to run the Side Post action or Short 17 Series.

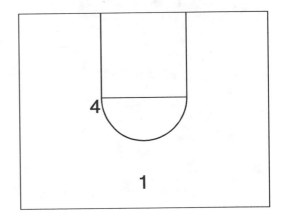

There are four parts to the Side Post action:

1) Pass, screen-and-roll

2) Dribble, screen-and-roll

3) Side post delay

4) Inside screen

Pass, Screen-and-Roll

If 2 doesn't receive the ball, 1 and 4 execute the screen-and-roll (left). 5 flashes to the junction of the foul line and lane line and we are in our continuity. (See Page 42)

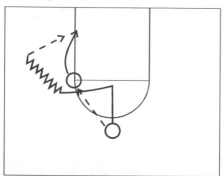 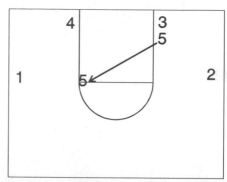

In the Pass, Screen-and-Roll, the ball is passed to a teammate (above) who then sets a screen as he hands the ball back to the first player rolling to the basket (below).

Dribble, Screen-and-Roll

Instead of passing the ball to 4, 1 dribbles into the top of the key and around the screen set by 4. 4 then rolls to the basket to take the pass from 1.

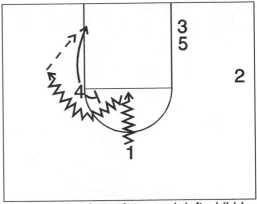

In the photo, the point guard, left, dribbles toward the forward who sets a screen in the Dribble, Screen-and-Roll drill.

Side Post Delay

1 passes to 4 then V-cuts and comes off 4 and does not get the pass back. 4 makes an inside pivot and fakes a pass to 2 but gives the pass to 1 then V-cuts and flashes down the lane.

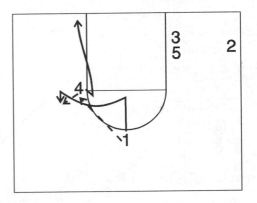

4 also can pass to 2 off the double screen (left, below). If 2 gets the ball, we "pop the stack" and are in our continuity (right, below). (See Page 42)

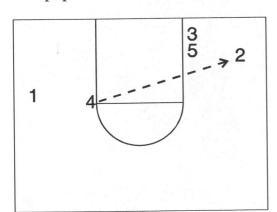

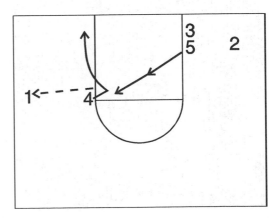

Side Post Delay

In the photos above, the forward fakes to the player coming off the double screen. The guard V-cuts and steps back. At left, the forward passes to a guard. He then V-cuts and dives to the basket.

Inside Screen

1 sets an inside screen for 4. 4 takes 1 dribble inside the foul line for a shot.

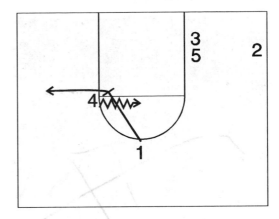

If he has no shot, he can pass to 2 and "pop the stack." (See Page 39.)

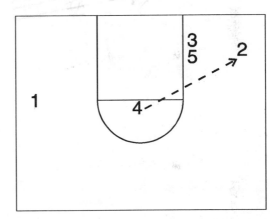

Or he can pass to 1 and V-cut to basket with 5 flashing.

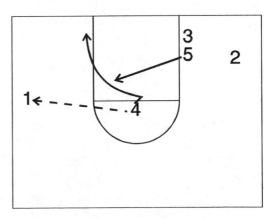

Inside Screen

(1)

(2)

In Photo No. 1, Player No. 1, left, sets an inside screen for Player No. 4 (with ball). Photo No. 2 shows No 4 dribbling to the free-throw line (Photo No. 3) where he can take a shot or pass to Player No. 2 on the right wing. He can also pass to Player No. 1 on the left wing and then V-Cut to the basket (Photo 4).

(3)

(4)

Pop the Stack

Double screens are an important ingredient of the balanced court high-post offense. There are a lot of double screens set for our players. We tell them the offense will get them a shot, but they have to make it.

When a player comes off the double screen and receives the ball on a pass, our players execute what we refer to as "Pop the Stack." There are several ways to "pop," but most of the time we place our center at the top of the stack. We want the bottom player to place his foot on the block with the top player beside him. They lean toward each other, pressing shoulder-to-shoulder so the defender is not able to get through the double screen.

In "Pop the Stack," the center is on top of the "stack" as shown here. The bottom player has his foot on the block. They lean toward each other so their shoulders touch, making it impossible for a defensive player to get through. This allows the player receiving the pass to get free when he goes to the basket (above) or when he goes to the wing.

Pop the Stack

There are many possibilities when you "Pop the Stack." The center can screen the forward's man and post up as the forward flashes up the lane (above), and a three-man game can be run (below).

Pop the Stack Drills

Objective:

This drill is designed to teach the proper technique of setting and using a double screen on the baseline, as well as screening the screener once the ball has been received by the cutter.

Teaching Points:

The post men share the block with their feet and create a solid screen by touching shoulders. The cutter learns to curl or flatten depending on whether the defender goes over (flatten) or under (curl) the screen.

Procedure:

   The guard starts under the basket. As the pass is made from the point to the wing (1), the guard V-cuts as the forward and center set a screen on the block. When the guard receives the pass, he dribbles to improve the angle as the center screens down for the forward who slides up the lane (2). This drill can be done either with or without the defense in place.

(1)

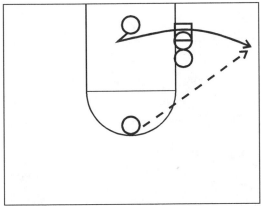

(2)

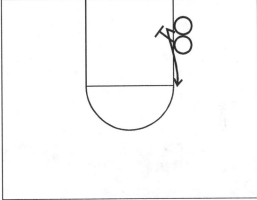

If a player coming off a double screen receives the ball, we pop the stack.

The center screens the forward's defender and posts up. The forward flashes up the lane and the guard moves to the free-throw line extended.

(3)

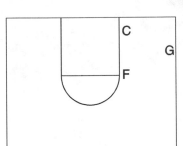

Three-man game

(4)

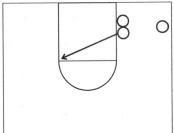

If a player coming off a double screen does not receive the ball, the center flashes to the opposite junction of the free-throw line and foul lane (elbow).

(5)

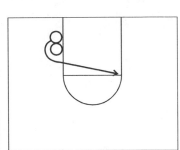

If you prefer, the bottom man could flash to the junction instead of the top man.

41

Continuity

The continuity of our offense is the area that almost all of our plays end up developing in. If we really share the ball and make the extra pass we will eventually end up in this set.

The center cannot pass to the forward and passes to the guard. The forward on his side posts up and the center screens down as the weakside forward V-cuts and comes up the lane.

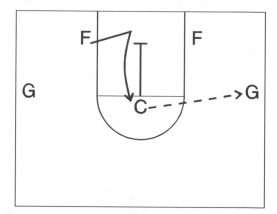

Continuity Alignment

If the guard can't give the ball to the post-up player, he passes to the forward coming up the lane and we repeat the action upon ball reversal.

The guard is always V-cutting.

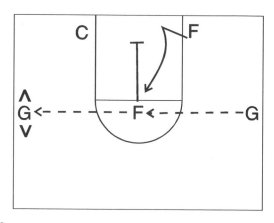

42

This is almost an offense by itself. You can screen-and-roll (left) or you can lob (right).

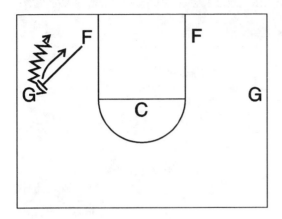 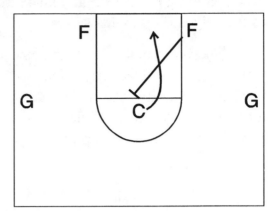

You can reverse the action ...   or ...

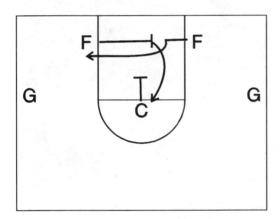 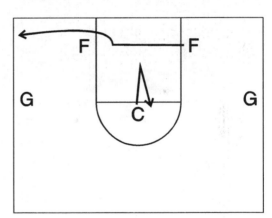

The high-post player passes to the wing while the strongside player posts up. The weakside player V-cuts off the screen to look for a 15-foot jump shot.

Again, the real beauty of the high-post offense is the flexibility it allows for you to design your own plays that fit your personnel.

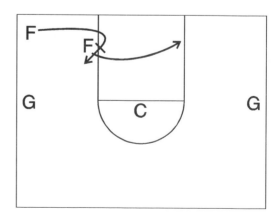

3

Alignment in the High-Post Offense

The development of the plays depends on the moves of the guard:

- Guard Cut
- Guard Backdoor
- Guard Hit Post
- Guard Dribble

- Guard Screen
- Guard Follow
- Guard Around
- Foward Reverse
- Guard Loop

1 and 2 align near the top of the key one step outside the lane line and either one or two steps above the top of the key which is the operational area. 3 and 4 should be 4 feet inside the sideline, while 5 is at the foul line, one step toward the strong (ball) side. (Diagram 1)

Make sure your players are spaced about 12 to 15 feet apart at all times. We feel spacing is the most important area in basketball offense. (Diagram 2)

Anything can go in the offense. It's designed to get the open shot. If you have a shot as good or better than one the offense provides, take it.

(1)

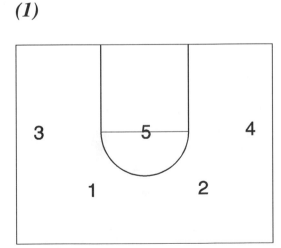

(2)

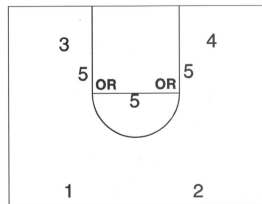

We start like this.

Examples:

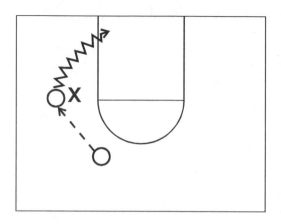

1. The forward is being overplayed. When he receives the ball, he either pivots or crosses over and drives to basket.

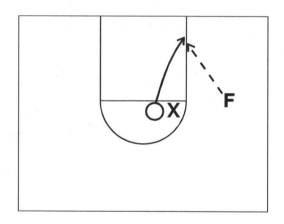

2. When the center is being denied ball, he reverse pivots and goes to basket.

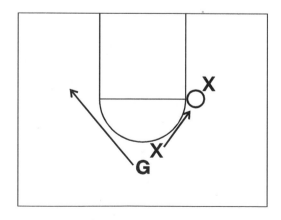

3. The center is double-teamed by the weakside guard's man. The weakside guard must go to the foul line extended and ask for the ball.

Vital Points

- All five men must move at all times, especially the weakside players, to keep their men busy.

- Fake away and give hand targets to ask for the ball.

- Start the offense with a guard-to-guard pass.

- The ball must not stick in the hands. Movement by the ball and the players must be very sharp and crisp.

- Use short, sharp, crisp passes.

- Plays can be run on either side of court. The guards and forward must be able to work either side.

Guard Cut

The guard cut is the "bread and butter" of the UCLA offense. Its unlimited options, each of which is determined by the forward's pass after he receives the entry pass from the guard, makes it an entire offense within itself. Anything can go in the offense which is designed to get the open shot. But if a player can get a better shot than the offense provides, he or she should take it.

Examples

- The forward being overplayed and receives the ball can either pivot or cross over and drive to the basket.
- A center being denied the ball can reverse pivot and go to the basket.

Other plays that we run from the high-post set are guard follow, guard around, guard screen and guard dribble No. 1 and No. 2. Our pressure releases are hit the post, backdoor and guard dribble. All players are moving constantly during every play, and all plays are keyed by the guard's initial movement.

Guard Cut

As 2 passes to 3, 5 turns and sets a backscreen. 4 drifts to block at the low post as 1 fakes away and comes head up on the basket about 4 feet from the top of the key. 2 will run to 5 and make a jab fake right or left and go either side. If 2 doesn't get the ball by the time he is one step from the block, he drifts to the baseline and 5 steps back to the ball.

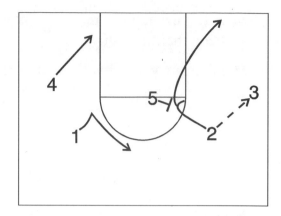

At this point, 3 has three options:

1. If he hits 2, 3 then sets screen on 5's man, pivots and rolls to the basket. 5 jabs and comes off the screen, and either shoots or passes to 1 or 2 and gets into continuity.

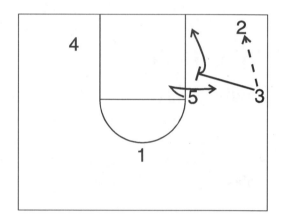

2. If 3 hits 5 on the baseline, 3 goes to the low-post block and jump stops. 2 ducks under the basket and comes off 3's screens. 3 pivots and faces 5 as 4 shapes up in the key on the weak side (duck move). 5 first tries to make eye contact with 4 then looks to 2 coming off the screen. 1 goes to the foul line extended on the weak side to set up continuity.

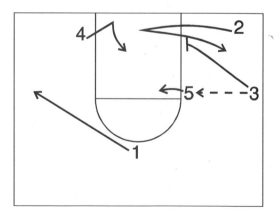

3. If 3 hits 1, 4 will come up the lane and jump stop out of the lane with one foot in and one foot out of the top of the key area. 1 and 4 run a side post while 5 and 3 set a double screen for 2 who ducks under the basket. 1 can run a side post or hit 2 off a double screen. If 2 gets the ball, 5 screens 3's man. 3 pops up the lane and 5 posts up. If 1 and 4 run a side post action after 4 vacates the side area, 5 flashes there. 5 and 3 can pop the stack but only if the player coming off the double screen receives the ball. 5 flashes to junction of the free-throw line and foul lane.

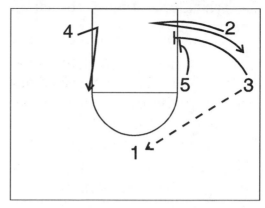

If 1 hits 4, see side post action. If 1 hits 2, we pop the stack.

Option No. 1 — Hit the Center (example)

After the center does proper footwork, 3 passes to him and sets a single screen for 2 on the baseline. 5 looks for 4 making a duck move then looks for 2 coming off 3's screen.

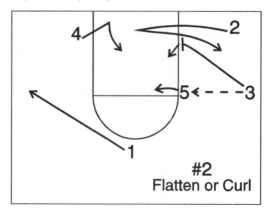

#2
Flatten or Curl

After 5 passes to 2 he screens away and we have our triangle continuity.

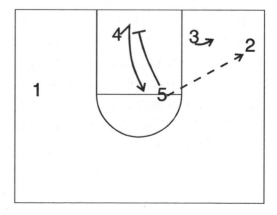

51

Triangle continuity formation (see continuity).

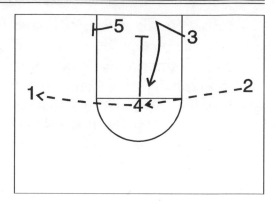

Option No. 2 — Hit Guard Out Front, Set Double Screen

If 3 passes to 1 up high he then sets a double screen with 5 for 2 and 4 comes up the lane for a side post.

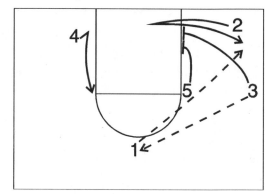

If 1 hits 2, 3 and 5 "pop the stack." 4 floats back down to the block and 1 goes to the opposite wing.

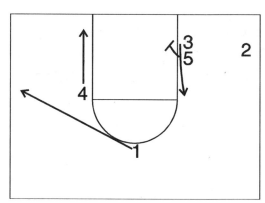

Triangle continuity.

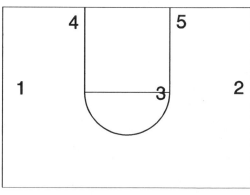

Option No. 3 — Hit the Guard Out Front

If 3 passes to 1 out front, 2 comes off the baseline double screen looking for a shot and 4 slides to the elbow. If 1 hits 4 with the pass, he then cuts off at the side post. (See four parts of side post action.)

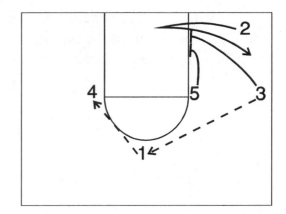

4 squares up to the basket, passes to 1 then jab fakes and cuts to the hoop looking for a return pass in a side post delay.

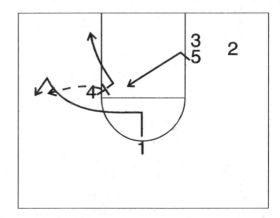

If the pass is not made to 4 cutting to the basket, we're in our triangle continuity formation.

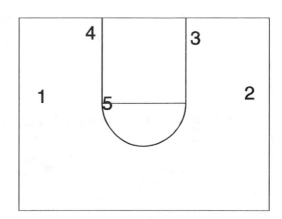

Option No. 4 — Hit the Guard on the Baseline

If 3 hits 2 on the baseline he sets a screen for 5 and rolls to the basket. 5 will V-cut before using the screen by 3 for a jump shot.

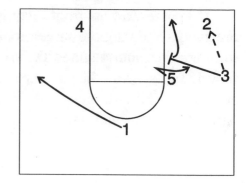

Continuity.

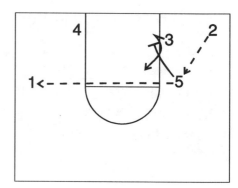

When you hit the guard on the baseline, you can do other things such as what is shown here where 4 backscreens for a lob.

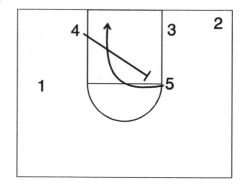

Or design your own option like the one shown here.

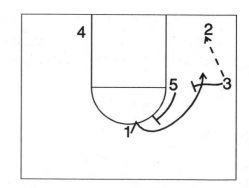

Guard Backdoor — Pressure Release

If the forward (4) sees a gap between the guards and the post, he takes two steps to the basket and bursts to the area at the top of the key.

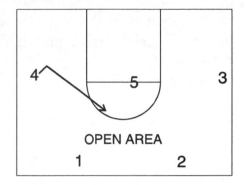

Here, 2 passes to 4 as 1 drives by 4.

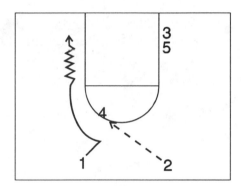

At this point, 2 fakes away and follows 1. 5 and 3 set a weakside double screen as 4 makes a drop-bounce pass to 1.

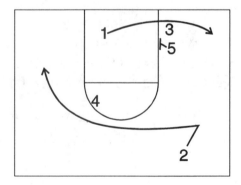

If 4 can't hit either 1 or 2, he pivots and faces the basket. 1 comes off the double screen and 2 flares out. If 4 hits 1, 5 and 3 pop the stack.

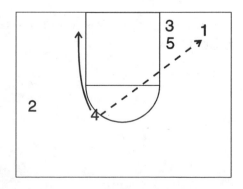

If 4 hits 2, 4 fakes away and bursts to the low post while 5 moves to the junction of the foul lane and foul line. If 5 receives a pass from 2, 3 runs a duck-in.

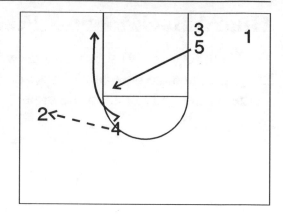

We are now in our continuity.

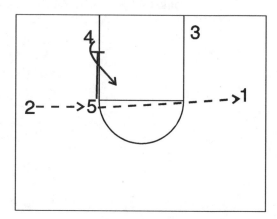

Guard Backdoor over the Top

Instead of passing to 4, 2 throws a lob to 1 who is cutting off 4.

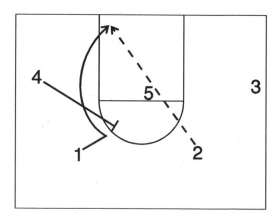

Hit Post — Pressure Release

All four plays are good.

2 passes to 5; 2 and 1 cross.

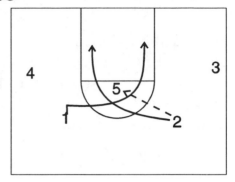

2 passes to 5, but this time the forwards, 3 and 4, cross.

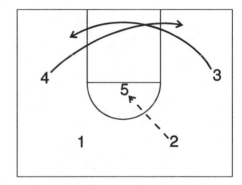

The guards, 1 and 2, cut and come off forward screens.

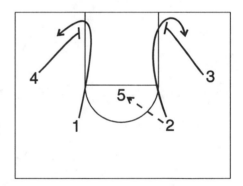

The guards cut and screen for the forwards.

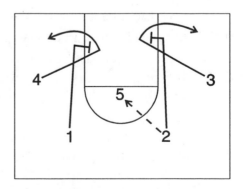

Guard Dribble — Pressure Release

1 dribbles directly at 3 who plants and goes backdoor. We like for him to catch the ball and take no more than one dribble and jump stop behind the block for a shot.

If that doesn't develop . . .

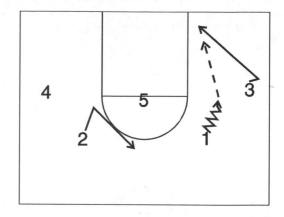

. . . 5 goes down the key, sets a screen for 4 and proceeds to the block. 3 sets the second leg of a double staggered pick for 4 who comes off both picks and posts up.

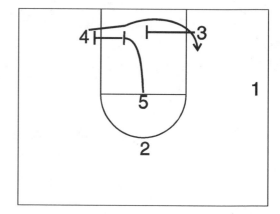

3 and 5 set a double screen. If 1 can't hit 4, he passes to 2. 4 reverses to come off the double screen and 1 goes down the lane and comes up for a 1-2 side post option. 1 can also post up and 2 can flash past him. If 2 hits 4, 3 and 5 pop the stack. If he hits 1, 4 is the safety.

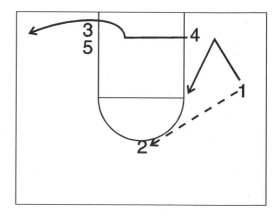

Options for the Weakside Guard Dribble Action

1 and 2 run a side post

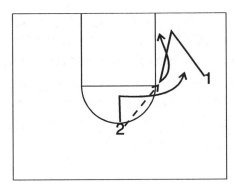

1 posts up

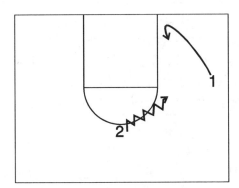

2 posts up

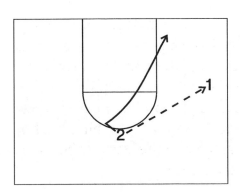

Guard Screen

1 hits 3 and screens for 2 who breaks for the basket for a layin off screens by 1 and 5 (left).

If that doesn't develop, then 4 and 5 go on the block away from the cutter while 3 passes to 1 who has stepped back to the front of the basket and 3 sets up on the block. 2 stays in the center of the lane. He fakes one way and comes off either a single or a double screen. If 2 comes off 3, he can shoot or hit 3 posting while 5 flashes to the junction (right).

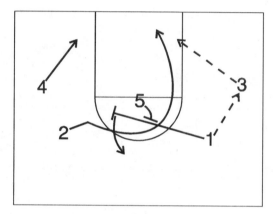
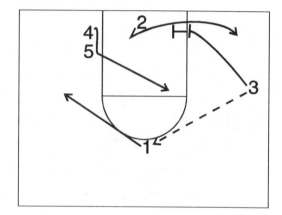

If 2 comes off 4 and 5, he can shoot or pass inside where 4 and 5 have popped the stack (left). But if 2 can do neither (on either side), he hits 1 (right). If on the weak side, 1 runs a side post with 3 or with 4 if 5 has cleared. If the pass comes to either side, we are in our continuity.

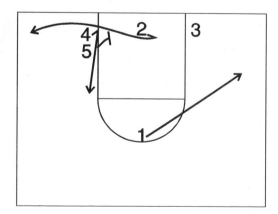
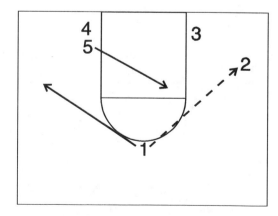

We also like to run a guard screen straight up. We just call screen and as the guard is bringing the ball up court, the players get into the alignment.

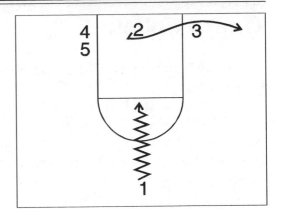

We like to run this from the other end of the floor with 6 or 7 seconds left on the clock.

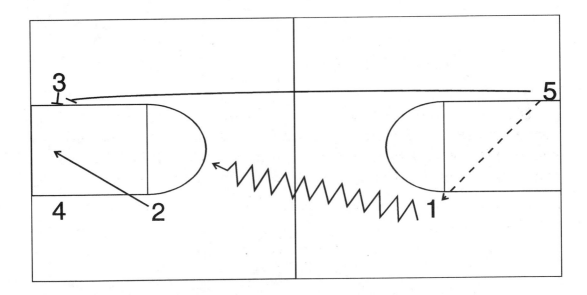

Guard Follow

1 passes to 3 and follows his pass to get the ball back. As 5 sets a screen at the junction of the free-throw line and foul lane, 4 bursts across the lane to the low post on the ball side. After he gives the ball back to 1, 3 goes over the top of 5's screen while 2 stays at home.

5 then continues out (right) and sets a screen for 1 who takes a three-bounce dribble off of it while 2 screens down for 3. After setting a screen for 1, 5 pivots and screens down for 4.

1 can now shoot or pass to 3 or 4, 2 if they switch, or 5 if he posts and flashes open. There is no continuity. 3 must come up the lane while 4 flattens out along the baseline.

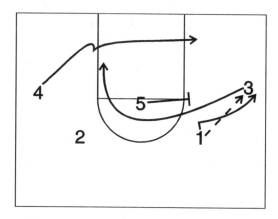
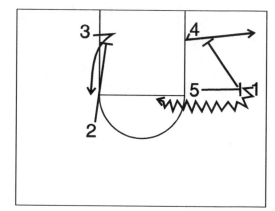

Guard Around

This is a continuation of the guard follow.

If the forward — either 3 or 4 — doesn't give the ball back to the guard, he continues around the screen to the block (left) where 5 sets a double screen with 2. 1 fakes away and comes head up on the basket to receive a pass from 3.

After 5 and 2 set the double screen (right), 4 goes low off of it as 3 comes high over the top.

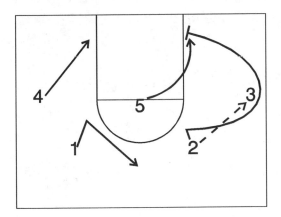
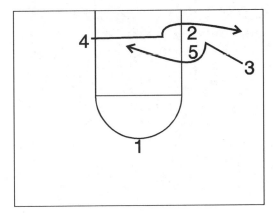

If 1 passes to 4, 2 and 5 pop the stack. If 1 passes to 3, he should be open. The continuity is with 2, 5 and 3. If 1 hits 4, we pop the stack and get into continuity. Either 1 or 4 is the safety.

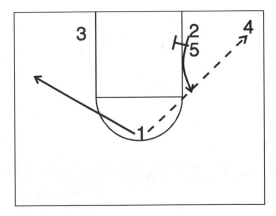

Forward Reverse

1 passes to 3 and 5 backscreens for 2 (left). 2 bursts off 5's screen to the basket and looks for a layin.

5 and 1 come together and set a double screen for 4 (right). 4 comes off the double screen for a shot at the foul line. 1 is the outside player on the screen and 5 is on the inside.

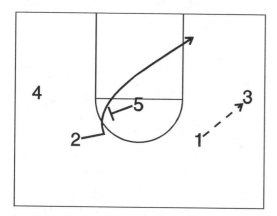
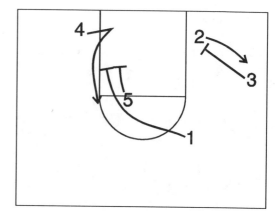

3 can pass to 2 for a shot or to 4 (left). As 1 breaks to the wing 3 and 2 interchange (right). We are now in continuity.

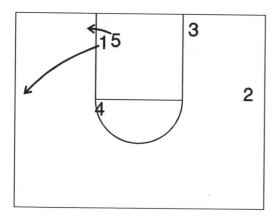
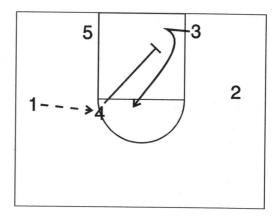

Guard Loop

1 passes to 2 then runs a cut by 5 and loops around to be head up on the basket at the top of the key. This is the same position he would be in if he were the weak guard.

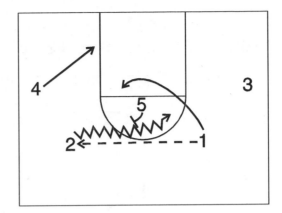

3 flares under the basket to the free-throw line extended on the other side and 4 goes to the block on his side. 5 sets a screen at top of key for 2 who dribbles off while 5 rolls.

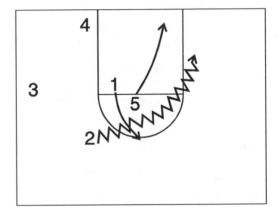

If 2 has no shot, he looks to 5 or can reverse ball to 1 who hits 3 who powers into 4 posted up. 1 screens down for 5.

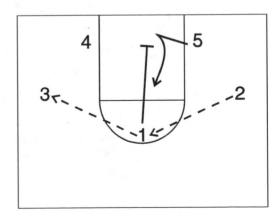

2 Up

2 passes to 4 and cuts to the free-throw line and then down to the baseline while 3 comes across to the opposite corner (left).

1 replaces 3 and 5 downscreens for 2 who comes up the lane (right).

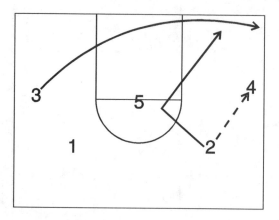
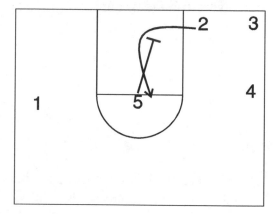

Center — Get Ball

4 goes to the block while 5 moves to the wing to receive the pass from 2. 2 then moves to the corner (left). 1 moves away and 3 flashes to the side post (right).

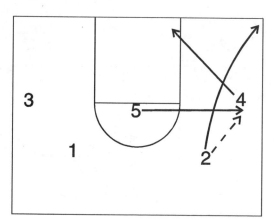
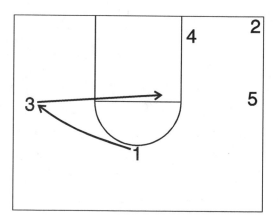

5 to 4
5 to 2 to 4
5 to 3 to 4
5 to 1 to 4

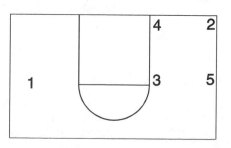

Set

2 dribbles out to 4 and as 5 drops to the short corner (left), 4 goes to screen for 3. 2 to 5 to 3.

2 to 1 for Side Post Action (right).

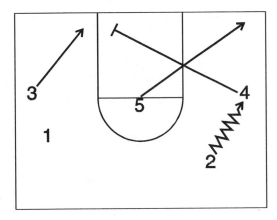 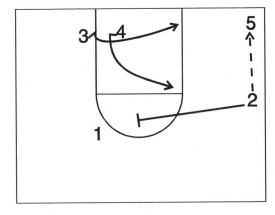

Side Post Split

2 passes to 4 (left) then cuts down through the lane to the opposite side and back out.

4 passes to 5 (right), and 4 and 1 complete the split.

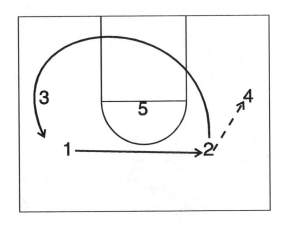 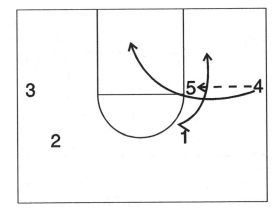

Post Center

Try to get the ball to 5, 4 or 2.

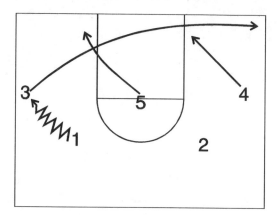
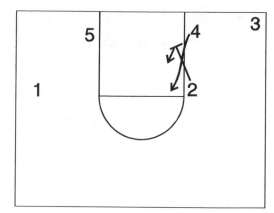

1 passes to 3 then cuts to the baseline setting up a shot for 3 or a drive for 5.

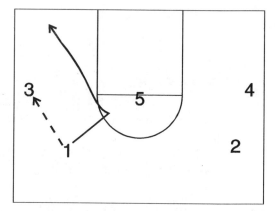

3 passes to 5 (left) then sets a double screen with 1 and 5 can drive to the basket, pass to 4, or pass to 1 and post up.

If 4 gets the ball, 1 and 3 pop the stack (right).

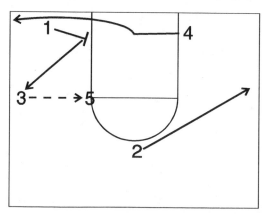
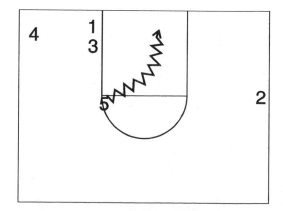

4

Drills to Teach the Balanced Court High-Post Offense

Forward Duck In (or Step-Through) Drills

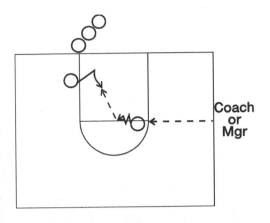

The center works on four steps. The forward V-cuts and steps through or ducks in. We try to develop eye-to-eye contact with the center and forward. Make a one-step or one-bounce dribble and make a below-the-knee bounce pass.

After receiving the pass (top photo), the player turns and either takes a step or a one-bounce dribble, then makes a below-the-knee bounce pass (bottom photo).

X defends the duck move. The guard has moved to the wing on the pass to post. The center can't pass to the post and passes to the wing. The forward pins or seals the defense while the guard makes one dribble to the endline and passes to the post.

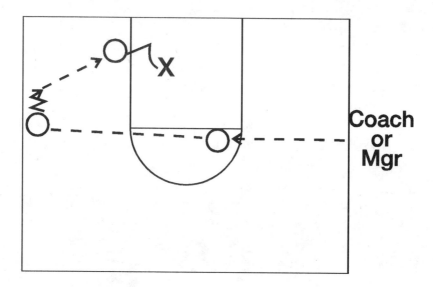

Defense can be added to this drill as shown here.

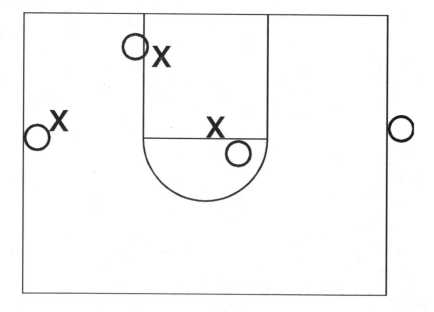

Side Post

We line up and run our four sidepost series plays, alternating one side each time. This drill covers ballhandling, passing, dribbling, catching, V-cuts, asking for the ball, shooting, rebounding, cutting and moving. Approximate length: 3 to 5 minutes.

Objective:

To teach the proper technique necessary to execute the sidepost option of our offense.

Teaching Points:

Forwards must break to the elbow hard and quick. They should have one foot in and one out of the circle, facing the intersection of the sideline and half-court line. Guards must make crisp passes and V-cut below the foul line. From here he has four options: Pass, screen-and-roll; dribble, screen-and-roll, inside screen and sidepost delay.

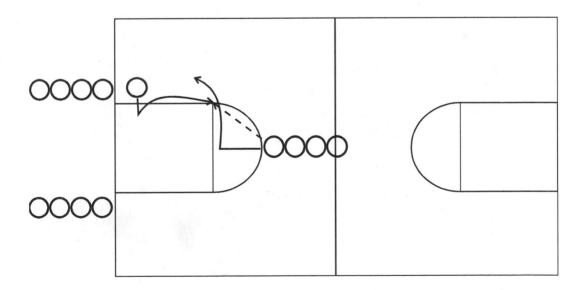

Procedure:

Frontline players start at the baselines and break up to the side post. The guards are in line near the top of the key and make a pass to the side post.

Pass, Screen-and-Roll

The guard passes to the forward, goes inside the top of the key and V-cuts off the forward. The forward gives the ball to the guard who takes one bounce as the forward rolls to the basket.

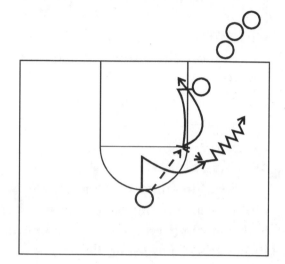

Dribble, Screen-and-Roll

The guard dribbles inside the top of the key and off the forward. The forward turns, faces the guard and screens for him, then rolls to the basket.

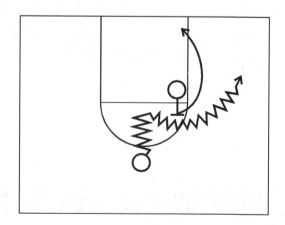

Side Post Delay

The guard passes to the forward and V-cuts as he did in the Pass, Screen-and-Roll. He comes off the forward and does not get the ball. He continues, V-cuts and steps back to foul line extended. The forward reverse pivots and fakes to the player coming off the double screen. He then passes to the guard, V-cuts and dives to the basket.

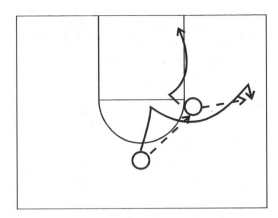

Inside Screen

The guard passes to the forward then goes to the free-throw line, sets an inside screen and flashes to free-throw line extended. The forward takes a one-bounce dribble to the middle of the free-throw line, looks for a shot or to the player off the double screen. He passes to the guard then V-cuts and dives to the basket.

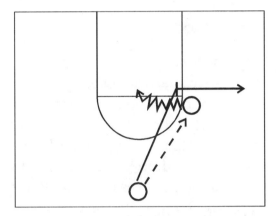

Pressure Release Drills

Guard Dribble

The forward comes out, plants his foot and backcuts. He gets a bounce pass and shoots one step behind the block. Run this two times on each side.

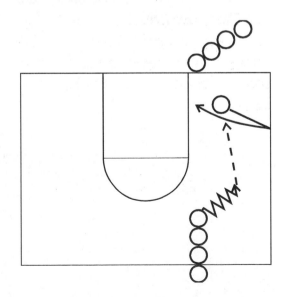

Hit the Post

The guard passes to the post and the forward executes the same backcut as in the Guard Dribble and receives a pass from the center. The forward stops behind the block and shoots a bank shot. Run two times on each side.

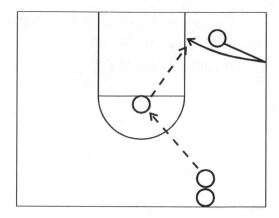

Backdoor

The forward comes to the wing, V-cuts and flashes to the top of the key. The opposite guard passes to the forward and the strongside guard V-cuts and rubs off the forward. The forward just drop-passes the ball to the guard who takes one dribble for a pull-up jumper off the glass. Run two times on each side. Approximate length: 5 minutes.

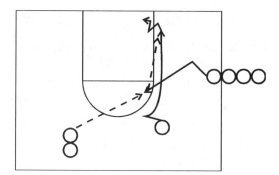

Pop the Stack

3 passes to 1 as 2 puts both feet into the lane and comes off a double screen set by 3 and 5.

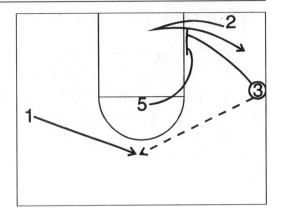

5 screens down for 3 to form a triangle on one side. 2 can pass to 5 posting or 3 for a high-low. 2 to 3 to 1 and screen down for 5.

Run several times on each side of the floor. Approximate length: 5 minutes.

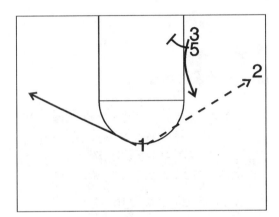

Downscreen

In our Guard Cut Series the guard ends up in the short corner. When the ball is passed to the high post, the guard works his man underneath the basket to set up his man for a downscreen.

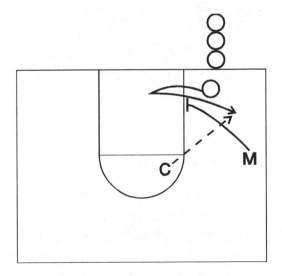

He comes off the screen and either "flattens out" or slightly curls depending on how the defense plays him. Try to have a manager or a coach play dummy defense on the guard.

The guard shoots, follows his shot and goes to the end of the line. Work both sides. ("M" is for manager; "C" is for coach.)

Hit the High Post and Flair

To release pressure our guards hit the high post, flair and spot up on the three-point line. We shoot three-point shots here and/or pump fake, take a one-bounce dribble and shoot.

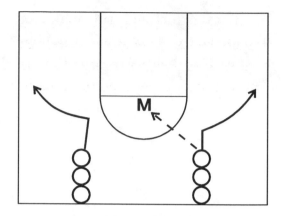

Guard Screen

This is where the shooter can take his man off either side. The guard at the top has the ball, reads which way the shooter goes and delivers a good pass. If there is defense on the shooter, he must flatten out or slightly curl to receive the pass and the passer becomes the next shooter. In both of these drills we teach our shooters to run their defenders into the screens.

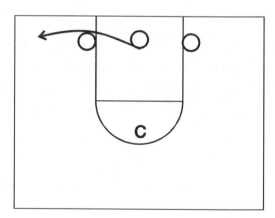

High-Post Screen

To get our guards to utilize the No. 2 play effectively, we have the guards drive hard off the screen, turn the corner and shoot the jumper or drive to the basket. Have the guards work off the high-post screen on both the left and right.

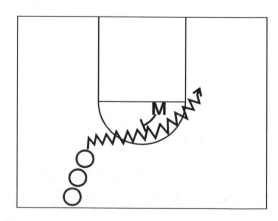

Hit the Low Post and Move

When we hit the low post, our players are taught to move to an open area, receive the pass back and shoot. You can shoot three-point shots in this drill.

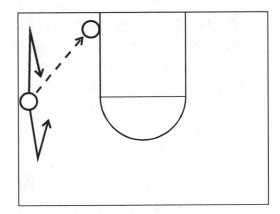

3-on-3 Strong Side with a Passer

Run this drill every day early in practice to work on getting the ball into the operational area. Getting the forward and center open and the guard cut can all be run from the high post in this drill.

This is a great offense versus defense drill that can be used to develop the single- or double-down screen for the guard. Other opportunities include posting up the forward, Pop the Stack, high-low, or having the center or forward pin or seal his defender.

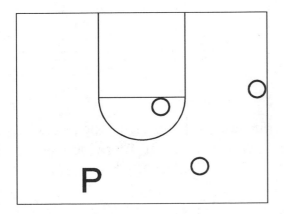

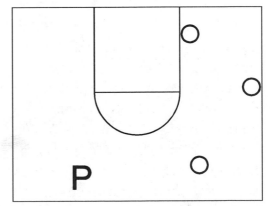

5-on-5 Strong Side

This drill is a continuation of the 3-on-3 strong side. All of your offense can be incorporated in this drill but it's better to concentrate on one phase at a time.

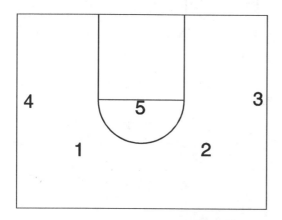 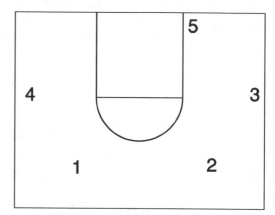

5-on-5 Controlled Scrimmage

The O's run a man-to-man offense. If they score, they press. If they don't score, they run a transition defense. The X's run a man-to-man defense.

If the X's are scored on, they run a press offense, but if the X's stop the O's, they run their fast break the full length of the court. If the X's score or O's rebound, stop play and turn it over.

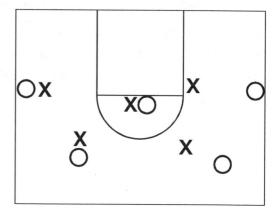

There is a great amount of coaching that goes into this drill which lasts 10 to 30 minutes and covers every aspect of your game. You can zone from it also.

5-on-0 Drill

The 5-on-0 Drill is a live, quick and fast drill we use to incorporate everything we want to accomplish in our offense. We run a play using the *Big 5* and *7 Areas of Improvement* (Chapter 1).

Try to make three to seven passes, shoot and always try to make the second shot. V-cuts, hands up, follow your shot are all used. After running one play, have five new players come in and run another. Players must learn to recognize that what the guard does reveals what play we will run. Mastering these skills will make a big difference in the way your team plays.

Approximate length: 10 minutes daily.

All five players must always be moving. Passes should be short, sharp and crisp. Work on triangle rebounding and having a medium and deep safety on every play.

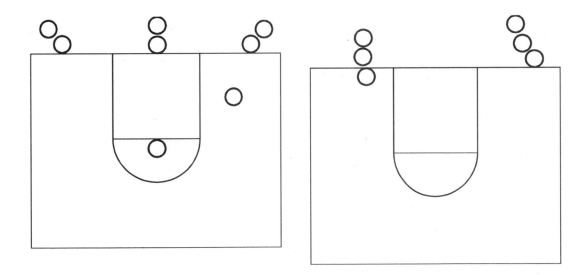

4-on-0 Drill with No Post

This is the same as the 5-on-0 except there is no post. A lot of your plays can be run this way and gives the players a different look.

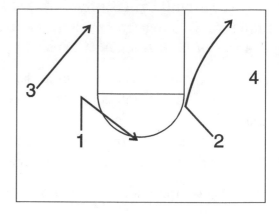

Guard Cut

Both guards make cuts. You can run any play imaginable but the single downscreen and side post are the most common.

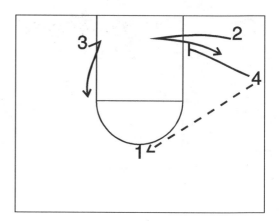

5

The Balanced Court Low-Post Offense

Guard Cut

1 passes to 3 and replaces 4. 4 goes to the junction of the foul line and foul lane.

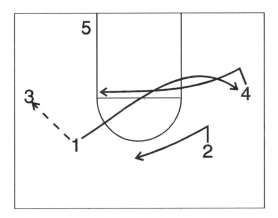

3 passes to 5 and then sprints to the basket. 4 comes off 3 for a split and 1 backscreens for 2.

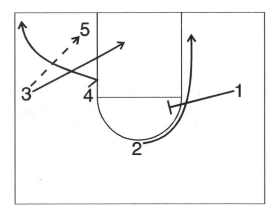

3 passes to 4. 4 can look for the high-low or reverse the ball to 1. 5 backscreens for 3.

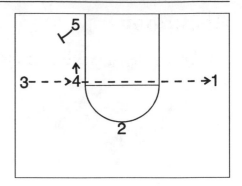

4 screens down for 5 and 2 replaces 3.

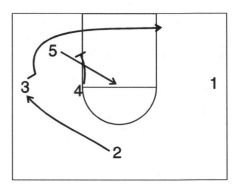

3 passes to 2 as 5 and 4 set a double screen.

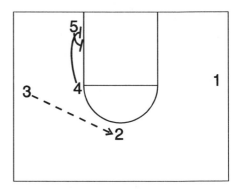

3 comes into the stack and goes over the top while 1 comes to the stack and goes underneath.

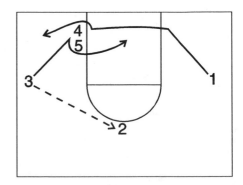

Backdoor

This is the same as the high-post backdoor.

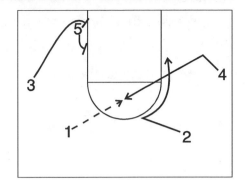

On the strong side of court 5 comes up to take a pass from 2 as 4 goes backdoor. 1 and 3 set a double screen and 2 comes off 5.

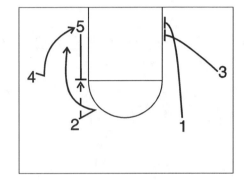

If nothing develops, 5 pivots and can pass to 4 off the double screen or to 2 and then flash to the basket.

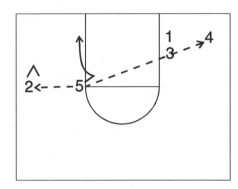

4 then flashes to the junction (left). 1 pops to the wing and we are in our continuity (right).

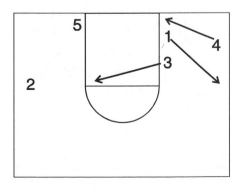
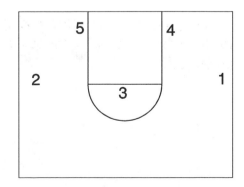

Guard Dribble

As 2 dribbles out, 4 and 5 set a double staggered screen for 3 (left). Now we are the same as the high post.

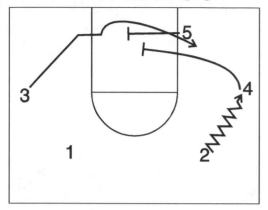 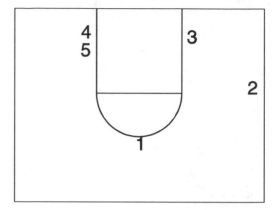

Guard Follow

2 passes to 4 who looks in to 5 as 3 flashes to the junction of the free-throw line and foul lane. After 2 passes to 4, he follows the pass and gets the ball back from 4 (left) and 4 goes over the top of 3 to the block (right).

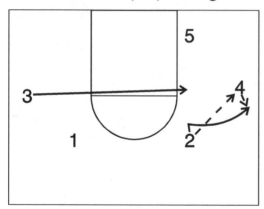 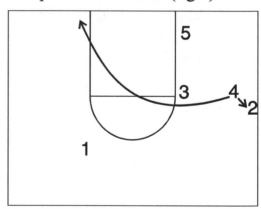

2 can then shoot or pass to 4 or 5. If switches occur on the defense, 2 can look for 1 or 3.

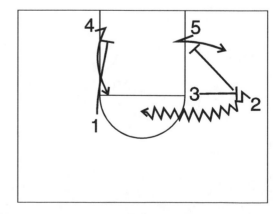

Guard Screen

This play is run exactly like the high post play. If 5 is low, 5 can move across the lane. If he is on the other side, just stay.

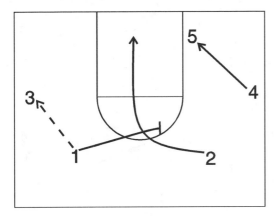
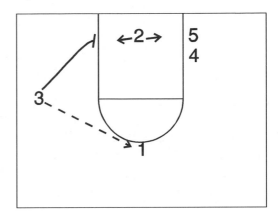

Guard Around

2 passes to 4 then goes around 4 to set a double screen with 5. 3 moves to the block and 1 goes to the top of the key (left).

4 and 3 move into 2 and 5's double screen at the same time (right). 4 comes over the top and 3 goes underneath. If 3 gets the ball, we "pop the stack."

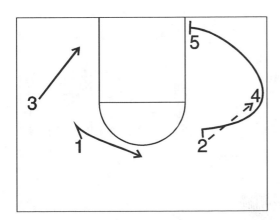
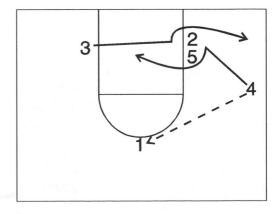

Corner Low or High

2 passes to 3 and sprints to the corner.

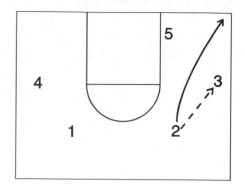

3 passes the ball back to 2 on the give-and-go.

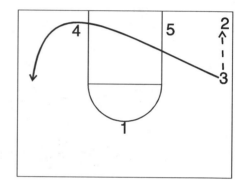

5 sets a screen-and-roll pick for 2 and 1, 4 and 3 spot up.

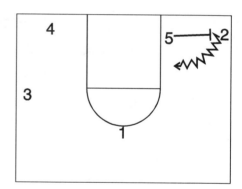

Option: 3 can also pass to 5 in the low post.

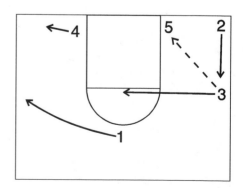

6

The Balanced Court Offense from a 1-2-2 Set

Guard Cut

1 passes to 2 and 5 backscreens 1's defender. This allows 1 to cut to the basket for a layin. If 1 doesn't get the ball he goes to the short corner. 3 replaces 1. (See the high-post guard cut.)

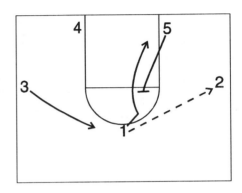

2 passes to 5 and 4 ducks in under the basket. 2 sets a downscreen for 1 as 3 goes to the opposite wing. 5 can now pass to 4 or 2 who screens and shows. If 5 hits 1, 2 downscreens for 4 and 5 downscreens for 2. (See the high-post guard cut.)

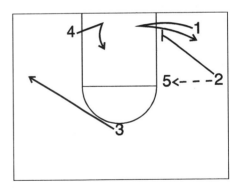

If 2 passes to 3, you can run the four sidepost options or pass to 1 off the double screen. Go away, 2 and 5 pop the stack and we are in our continuity. (See the high-post guard cut side post double down.)

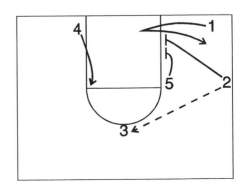

Hit the Post Backdoor — Pressure Release

1 enters the ball to 5 at the high post as 2 goes backdoor. 3 and 4 set a double screen on the opposite block and 1 runs a side post off of the high post.

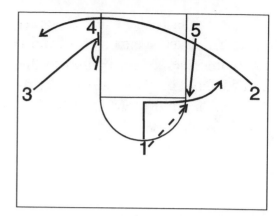

5 has two options:

1. He can pass to 2 who has come off the double screen. If he does, 3 pops the stack to the foul line and 5 slides down the lane to the opposite block and we are in continuity.

2. He can pass to 1, jab step away and dive to the basket as 4 flashes to the ballside high post and we are now into continuity.

(1)

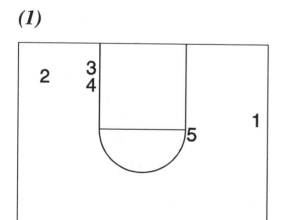

(2)

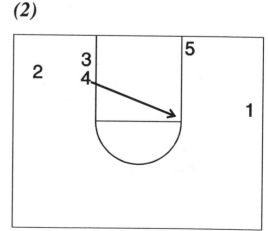

Guard Dribble — Pressure Release

1 dribbles to the wing. 2 begins to clear, 5 dives to the low post and 1 looks into the post. 4 flashes to the ballside high post. When 1 passes to 4 we have a high-low game with 4 and 5.

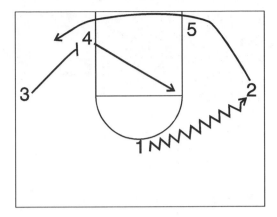

3 sets a single downscreen for 2 and 4 looks to hit 2 for the quick jumper.

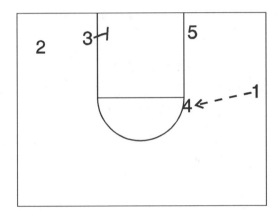

4 then downscreens away opposite and we are now in continuity.

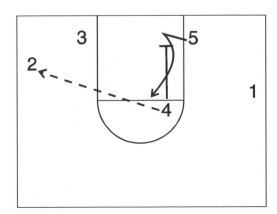

Offense "Weakside Clearout"

1 hits the wing and goes through to the ball side. 4 flashes to the high post and 2 immediately looks in to the block.

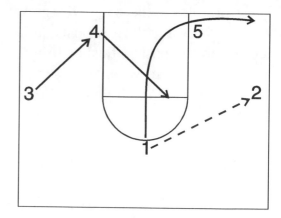

As the weak side clears out, the opposite wings go to the basket.

If 2 doesn't have the lob, he passes to 4 at the high post and 4 looks at 3 on the duck-in move.

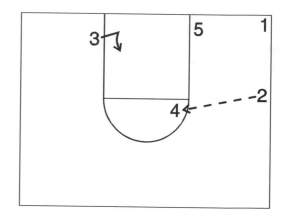

Option: 2 can also pass to 1 on the baseline and go through to the opposite wing and we are in continuity.

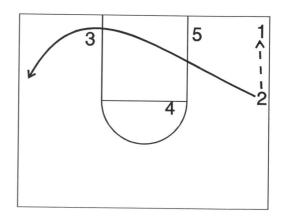

7

The
FIST Series

FIST Regular

1 has the option and the space to create opportunities by penetration. After passing to 2 on the wing, 1 goes through to the opposite side (left). 2 must first look immediately into the post. 5 flashes to the ballside high post coming right off of 1.

3 begins to move, ready to screen for 4 (right). 2 passes to 5 while 3 is screening for 4. After receiving the pass, 5 swings the ball to 1. 4 comes off the screen, preferably to the low side.

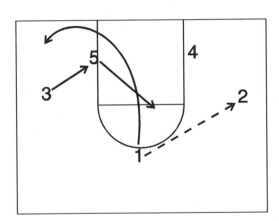

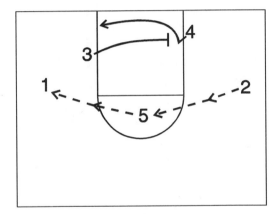

1 looks into 4 at the low post. 5 downscreens for 3 as 2 is spotting up behind the three-point line. We are now into continuity.

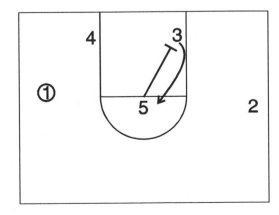

FIST in Transition

5 is the player who inbounds the ball. 4 is the pressure release and 2 and 3 run the lanes. 1 brings the ball to the middle of the floor with several options. 1 passes to 2 (left) and goes through as 4 plants hard and flashes to the low post. 5 is coming as the trailer and 3 is ready to cross-screen for 4. 2 passes to 5 who is behind the three-point line and 3 screens for 4 (right).

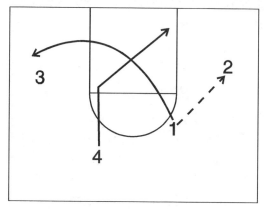

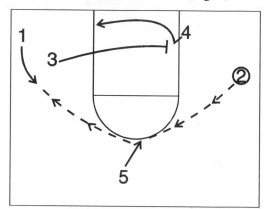

After 5 swings the ball to 1 who looks into the post for 4, 5 down-screens for 3 and we are right into continuity.

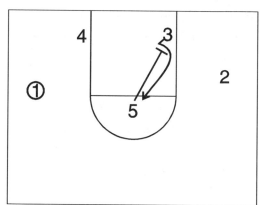

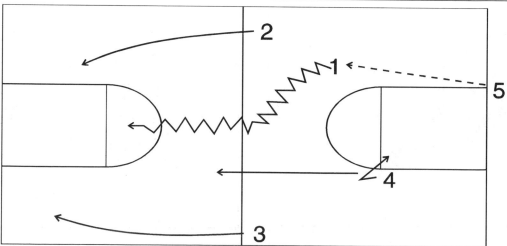

Play No. 1 from Fist Set

1 enters the ball to the wing opposite the best post shooter (left). 3 cheats in to form a double screen with 1 for 4. 3 is on the inside and 1 is on the outside. 2 looks to 5 or 4.

If 4 doesn't take the shot, 3 will post up on the block and 1 pops back to the wing (right). We have our continuity formation when 3 posts up. 4 passes to 1 and 1 looks at 3 as 4 screens down for 5.

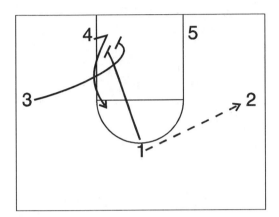 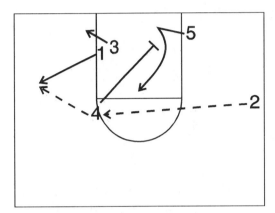

Play No. 2 from Fist Set

1 drives off a high screen set by 4 after 2 clears (left). 1 can then go to the basket ... or 1 can hit 4 rolling to the basket (right). If nothing develops, the ball is reversed and we are in continuity.

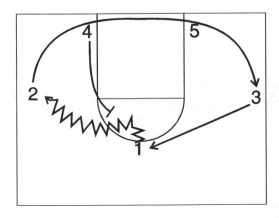 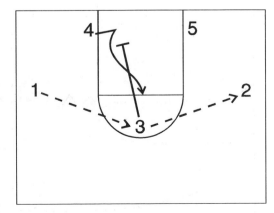

FIST to the "1-4" Flat Offense

Out of the 1-4 set we simply push the wings to the baseline and the forwards to the short corner. This is to be used when the shot clock has less than 10 seconds left and we want to open the floor for a quick penetrating point guard.

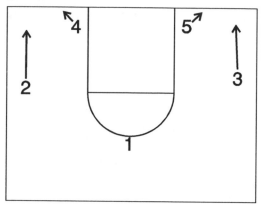 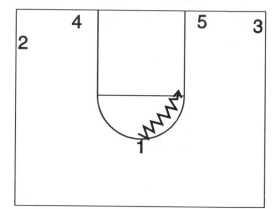

This is very effective with two shooters on the wings and two scoring forwards. It allows the point guard four options as he penetrates.

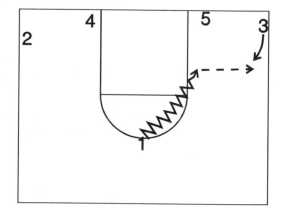

*The main responsibility of the point guard is to get into the paint. Be smart. Know your personnel and take what the defense gives you.

8

The
Box Set Series

Box Set A

1 must first take the ball away from the entry side to tighten up the defense. He dribbles to the wing in a position to enter the ball to the block. 3 sets a backscreen for 4 who comes off the screen on the back side to the block. 3 then flares to the wing behind the three-point line. 1 looks for 4 on the block (left). 5 then downscreens for 2 who comes up the lane for the 15-foot jumper (right).

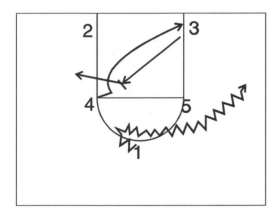

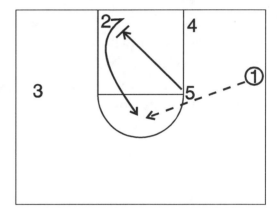

5 turns and pins looking for the ball. 2 looks in or swings the ball to 3 who looks in to 4. 2 then downscreens and we are now in continuity.

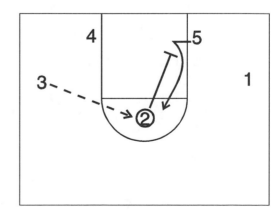

Box Set B

Begin in the same alignment as Box Set A. 1 must take the ball away from the direction he is going to tighten the defense. 2 cross-screens for 5.

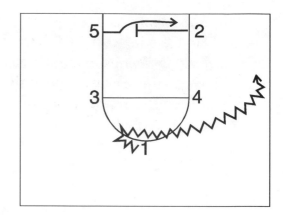

3 and 4 set a downscreen for 2 in the middle of the lane. 2 must come off the screen ready to score after receiving the ball from 1.

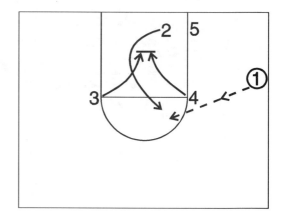

3 pops to the wing while 4 turns and pins, looking for the ball.

We are now in continuity.

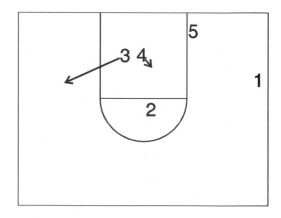

Box Set C

This is the same set as A and B. 1 dribbles to the wing and 2 steps to the basket and then pops to the short corner. 3, who has come off the cross screen, steps under the basket and then comes off a double screen set by 4 and 5.

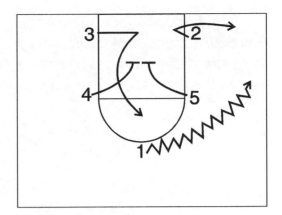

3 must use the screen and come off ready to score after receiving the ball from 1. 4 rolls to the basket from the ball side as 5 rolls down to the opposite side.

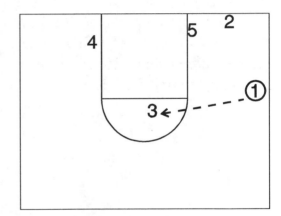

2 runs the baseline and spots up on the wing and we are now into continuity.

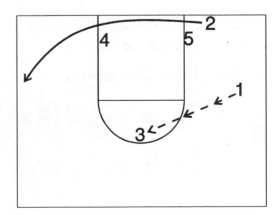

UCLA head coach Jim Harrick signals to his players from the bench. Harrick coached the Bruins to the 1995 national championship, UCLA's first title since John Wooden retired in 1975.

About the Author

Jim Harrick coached the UCLA men's basketball team to the NCAA championship in 1995. Since becoming the UCLA coach in 1988, the Bruins have been in the NCAA tournament every year, advancing to the final eight in 1992 and the final 16 in 1990. UCLA's title in 1995 was the first since 1975, legendary coach John Wooden's last season at UCLA after winning an unprecedented 10 national championships.

In seven years at UCLA, Harrick has compiled a record of 168 wins and 55 losses and led the Bruins to seven straight 20-win seasons, something not even Wooden was able to accomplish. After the 1995 season Harrick was named the Naismith and National Association of Basketball Coaches Coach of the Year, Pacific-10 Coach of the Year, honored as the American Youth Award's man of the year, and was given the coveted Spirit of Los Angeles Award by the Los Angeles Headquarters Association, an organization of 150 major corporations and businesses in greater Los Angeles.

Harrick was a highly successful coach even before coming to UCLA. At nearby Pepperdine, Harrick compiled a record of 167 wins and 97 losses in nine seasons from 1979-80 to 1987-88. His teams appeared in the NCAA tournament four times and the National Invitation Tournament twice, and Harrick was named West Coast Athletic Conference coach of the year four times.

Harrick began his coaching career at Inglewood's (Calif.) Morningside High School where he compiled a 103-16 record in four seasons. He later was an assistant at Utah State and later UCLA before taking the Pepperdine position. A native of Charleston, W. Va., Harrick is a 1960 graduate of the University of Charleston. He gave the commencement address there in 1994 and was awarded an honorary doctorate degree. He is a member of the school's Sports Hall of Fame and Alumni Gallery of Achievement.

In addition to his coaching duties, Harrick is one of the most respected clinic instructors in the United States and has traveled throughout the world as an American basketball goodwill ambassador, participating in clinics in China, Yugoslavia, Japan and Portugal. He led the Bruins on a two-week, nine-game playing tour of Italy in 1992 and was an assistant coach for the U.S. team that won the gold medal at the World University Games in 1993. He helped select U.S. players for the 1990 Goodwill Games and 1987 Pan-American Games.

UCLA coach Jim Harrick, right, talks with guard Tyus Edney during a break in game action.

UCLA center George Zidek stretches for a rebound during the 1994-95 season.

UCLA coach Jim Harrick greets Bruins center George Zidek during a game in the 1994-95 season.

More Basketball Books from Masters Press

Holding Court: *Reflections on the Game I Love*

by Dick Vitale with Dick Weiss

When Dick Vitale speaks out, sports fans listen. And speak out he does in this insightful new book, on everything from the baseball strike to the Simpson trial. As one of America's leading basketball analysts, Vitale concentrates on the sport he knows best and looks at the game from every angle. Drawing from his years as a college and NBA coach to his colorful commentary for ESPN and ABC, Vitale shares some of his insights and opinions about basketball's past, present and future. How has coaching changed? Who are the best coaches and what makes them great? Has the increased emphasis on academics made a difference? As more players leave school early, is recruiting getting out of hand? Does the NBA salary cap do what it was meant to do? Vitale looks at these and a host of other subjects including the return of Michael Jordan, television's impact on college basketball, and, of course, the NCAA tournament.

November • 256 pages • 6 x 9 • $22.95
B&W Photos • Cloth • 1-57028-037-1

Hoopla: *One Hundred Years of College Basketball*

by Peter C. Bjarkman

By all reasonable measures, basketball is the nation's favorite sport. More people watch basketball at the college, high school and professional levels than any other form of athletic competition. Despite increased popularity of professional basketball on TV, college basketball still has a firm grip on most basketball fans as the popularity of the NCAA tournament attests. *Hoopla: One Hundred Years of College Basketball* looks back at the game that evolved from a set of peach baskets nailed to the wall to today's slam-dunk, in-your-face, trash-talking version touching on the all-time great players, coaches, teams and moments along the way. This book will make it clear why college basketball has never had to yield to its professional competition.

January • 320 pages • 6 x 9 • $19.95
Photo insert • Cloth • 1-57028-039-8

These and other Masters Press books are available at most better bookstores or they may be ordered from Masters Press by calling: 800-722-2677.